Table of Contents

Introduction 1
Chapter 1: Introduction to Corporate Event Planning 4
Chapter 2: Assessing Your Skills and Qualifications 8
Chapter 3: Understanding Your Target Market. 12
Chapter 4: Developing Your Business Plan 18
Chapter 5: Legal and Regulatory Considerations 23
Chapter 6: Setting Up Your Business Operations 29
Chapter 7: Building Your Brand and Online Presence 34
Chapter 8: Acquiring Clients and Networking. 38
Chapter 9: Providing Exceptional Client Service. 43
Chapter 10: Growing Your Corporate Event Planning Business 49

Introduction

Welcome! I'm thrilled to have you join us on this journey through "The Ultimate Guide on How to Start a Corporate Event Planning Business." Whether you're a seasoned pro in event planning or a complete newbie looking to dive into this exciting industry, this guide is designed with you in mind. We'll walk you through every step, providing the knowledge and tools you need to build and grow your own successful corporate event planning business.

Starting a business can be a whirlwind of emotions—exciting, challenging, and incredibly rewarding. Corporate event planning is a field where you can transform your passion for organizing and managing events into a profitable venture. By delivering top-notch services, you can help businesses create unforgettable and successful events.

Let's begin by getting acquainted with the world of corporate event planning. In **Chapter 1**, we'll introduce you to the different types of corporate events, the crucial role of an event planner, and the unique benefits and challenges you might face in this industry.

Next, in **Chapter 2**, we'll help you assess your skills and qualifications. This chapter dives into the essential skills and attributes needed to thrive as an event planner and offers tips on how to develop and enhance these abilities.

Understanding your target market is vital for any business. **Chapter 3** will guide you through identifying your ideal clients. By grasping their needs, preferences, and pain points, you'll be able to craft event experiences that not only meet but exceed their expectations.

Chapter 4 focuses on developing a solid business plan. We'll walk you through creating a comprehensive roadmap that outlines your mission, target market, marketing strategies, financial projections, and more. A well-thought-out business plan is your blueprint for success.

Legal and regulatory considerations are a must when starting any business. In **Chapter 5**, we'll cover the legal requirements and regulations specific to the event planning industry. We'll discuss business licensing, insurance, contracts, and other legal aspects to ensure your business and clients are protected.

In **Chapter 6**, we'll dive into the nuts and bolts of setting up your business operations. From choosing the right business structure to establishing your office space and acquiring the necessary equipment, this chapter covers the practical steps to get your business up and running smoothly.

Building a strong brand and online presence is crucial in today's digital age. **Chapter 7** explores strategies for branding your event planning business and creating an effective online presence through websites, social media, and other marketing channels.

Acquiring clients and networking are essential for growing your business. **Chapter 8** offers practical tips on marketing your services, building relationships with potential clients, and leveraging networking opportunities to expand your client base.

Exceptional client service is the cornerstone of any successful business. **Chapter 9** delves into best practices for delivering outstanding service that not only meets but exceeds client expectations, fostering long-term relationships.

Finally, in **Chapter 10**, we'll look at strategies for scaling your business. From expanding your services and collaborating with industry professionals to adapting to market trends, this chapter will help you grow and sustain your corporate event planning business.

Throughout this guide, you'll find practical tips, real-life examples, and actionable insights to help you navigate your entrepreneurial journey. Get ready to unleash your creativity, make a meaningful impact, and embark on an exciting path in the world of corporate event planning.

Chapter 1: Introduction to Corporate Event Planning

Welcome to the first chapter of "The Ultimate Guide on How to Start a Corporate Event Planning Business." In this chapter, we'll embark on an exciting journey into the fascinating world of corporate event planning. Together, we'll explore what this industry is all about and give you a comprehensive overview of what you can expect.

What is Corporate Event Planning?

Corporate event planning is a specialized niche within the broader event planning industry. It focuses on organizing and executing events specifically for businesses and organizations. These events can range from small, intimate team-building exercises and meetings to large-scale conferences, trade shows, product launches, and corporate retreats.

As a corporate event planner, your role is to ensure these events run smoothly, meet the client's objectives, and leave a lasting impression on attendees. This job requires a unique blend of skills, including impeccable organization, a keen eye for detail, creativity, and the ability to juggle multiple tasks at once.

The Importance of Corporate Events

Corporate events are crucial in the business world. They offer companies a chance to connect with clients, partners, employees, and the community. These events serve various purposes, such as strengthening relationships, creating brand awareness, launching new products, celebrating achievements, or simply fostering a positive company culture.

A successful corporate event can significantly impact a company's reputation, brand image, and bottom line. Therefore, businesses are more than willing to invest resources into planning and executing high-quality events that align with their goals and values.

The Benefits of Starting a Corporate Event Planning Business

Starting a corporate event planning business can be both exciting and rewarding for aspiring entrepreneurs. Let's explore some of the key benefits:

1. Lucrative Industry

The corporate event planning industry is highly profitable, with a steady demand for services. Companies are eager to invest in professional event planners to ensure their events' success. With the right skills and business strategies, you can generate substantial income in this field.

2. Flexibility

Running your own event planning business offers you significant flexibility in terms of working hours and location. You can choose the clients you want to work with and the types of events you prefer to organize. This flexibility allows you to create a work-life balance that suits your personal needs.

3. Creativity and Variety

As a corporate event planner, you'll have the chance to unleash your creativity and design unique experiences for your clients. Each event comes with its own set of challenges and requirements, ensuring that no two projects are the same. This variety keeps the job exciting and provides continuous opportunities for learning and growth.

4. Networking Opportunities

Working in the corporate event planning industry opens doors to valuable networking opportunities. You'll have the chance to build relationships with industry professionals, potential clients, and suppliers. Establishing a strong network can lead to referrals, partnerships, and future business opportunities.

In this chapter, we've introduced you to the world of corporate event planning and highlighted the benefits of starting your own business in this exciting field. In the next chapter, we'll dive deeper into assessing your skills and qualifications to ensure you're well-prepared for this rewarding endeavor. Stay tuned!

Chapter 2: Assessing Your Skills and Qualifications

Starting a corporate event planning business is an exciting journey, but it's essential to take a step back and thoroughly assess your skills and qualifications to ensure you're well-prepared for the challenges ahead. Understanding your strengths and areas for improvement will help you build a solid foundation for your business. Let's dive into the various aspects you should consider when evaluating your skills and qualifications for this industry.

Evaluating Your Event Planning Experience

First things first, reflect on your previous event planning experience. Think about any relevant work you've done in the past. Have you coordinated personal events, like family gatherings or weddings? Have you assisted in organizing community events or volunteered for event planning committees? All these experiences count. They provide a valuable foundation and help you understand the nuances involved in planning successful events. Even if your experience isn't directly related to corporate events, the skills and insights you've gained can be incredibly beneficial.

Identifying Transferable Skills

While having specific event planning experience is undoubtedly valuable, don't underestimate the importance of transferable skills. These are the skills that are not only relevant but crucial in the corporate event planning field.

Consider your organizational abilities—can you juggle multiple tasks efficiently? How about problem-solving—are you good at thinking on your feet when things don't go as planned? Communication skills are also vital, as you'll need to interact with clients, vendors, and team members effectively. Attention to detail ensures that no aspect of the event is overlooked, and the ability to multitask is essential when managing the various components of an event simultaneously. Assess your proficiency in these areas and think about how you can leverage these skills to meet the unique demands of corporate event planning.

Acquiring Knowledge and Education

To further enhance your skills and qualifications, you might need to acquire additional knowledge and education in event planning and related fields. Consider enrolling in courses or programs specifically tailored for event planners. These courses can provide you with insights into best practices, current industry trends, and effective event management techniques. Additionally, attending workshops, seminars, and conferences can offer valuable networking opportunities and deepen your expertise. The more you know, the better equipped you'll be to handle the challenges that come your way.

Building a Network

In any business, building a professional network is crucial, and corporate event planning is no exception. Start connecting with industry professionals. Attend networking events, join associations and organizations related to event planning, and seek mentorship from experienced individuals in the field. Your network can provide support, guidance, and open doors to collaboration opportunities and potential client referrals. Having a strong network can be a game-changer for your business.

Assessing Financial Resources

Assessing your financial resources is another critical aspect of starting your business.

Starting a corporate event planning business may require an initial investment in equipment, technology, marketing, and professional development. Evaluate your financial situation to determine if you have the necessary resources. If you find that you need additional funds, explore funding options such as loans or grants to support your business's growth. Being financially prepared will help you focus on building your business without unnecessary stress.

Conclusion

Assessing your skills and qualifications is a vital step in starting a successful corporate event planning business. Take the time to evaluate your event planning experience, identify your transferable skills, acquire the necessary knowledge and education, build a strong professional network, and assess your financial resources. By doing so, you'll be well-positioned for success and ready to navigate the challenges of the corporate event planning industry.

Next, we'll explore **Chapter 3: Understanding Your Target Market**. In this chapter, we'll delve into identifying your ideal clients and understanding their needs, preferences, and pain points to create tailored event experiences that exceed their expectations. Stay tuned!

Chapter 3: Understanding Your Target Market

Alright, let's dive into Chapter 3 of "The Ultimate Guide on How to Start a Corporate Event Planning Business." This chapter is all about understanding your target market. Trust me, knowing your target market inside and out is a game-changer. It determines the types of events you'll plan, the services you'll offer, and how you'll attract clients. So, let's explore why understanding your target market is so important and some strategies to help you connect with your ideal clients.

Why is Understanding Your Target Market Important?

Before you start marketing your services and trying to attract clients, you need to have a crystal-clear understanding of who your target market is. Why? Because when you understand your target market, you can tailor your services and marketing efforts to meet their specific needs and preferences. This not only helps you attract the right clients but also ensures you're providing real value and delivering exceptional event planning services.

Identifying Your Ideal Client

The first step in understanding your target market is identifying your ideal client. Think of your ideal client as the type of person or company you'd love to work with and who would benefit most from your services. When defining your ideal client, consider factors such as:

- **Industry:** What sectors do they operate in? Are they in tech, finance, healthcare, etc.?
- **Event Types:** Do they need conferences, product launches, team-building events, etc.?
- **Company Size:** Are you targeting small businesses, medium-sized enterprises, or large corporations?
- **Budget:** What is their budget range for events?
- **Geographic Location:** Where are they located? Are you focusing on local clients or expanding your reach?

Researching Your Market

Once you have a picture of your ideal client, it's time to do some market research. This step helps you gain a deeper understanding of your potential clients' needs, preferences, and pain points. Here are some ways to conduct market research:

- **Analyze Industry Trends:** Keep an eye on the latest trends and developments in the event planning industry.
- **Study Competitor Strategies:** Look at what your competitors are doing. What works for them? What doesn't?
- **Surveys and Interviews:** Conduct surveys or interviews with potential clients to get firsthand insights into their needs and challenges.

Segmenting Your Market

Your target market is likely to consist of different segments with unique characteristics and preferences. By segmenting your market, you can create tailored marketing efforts to reach specific groups within your target market. Consider factors such as:

- **Industry:** Different industries have different event planning needs.
- **Event Size:** Small, medium, or large events?
- **Budget:** Different segments may have different budget constraints.
- **Geographic Location:** Local, regional, national, or international focus?

By segmenting your market, you can craft targeted marketing messages and strategies for each segment.

Connecting with Your Target Market

Now that you have a clear understanding of your target market, it's time to develop strategies to connect with and attract them. Here are some tips to help you effectively reach and engage your target market:

1. Develop a Strong Online Presence

In today's digital age, having a strong online presence is crucial. Create a professional website that showcases your services, past events, and client testimonials. Utilize social media platforms to share engaging content, interact with potential clients, and build relationships within your industry.

2. Attend Industry Events and Network

Networking is a powerful tool in the event planning industry. Attend industry events, trade shows, and conferences to connect with potential clients and industry professionals. Build relationships, exchange business cards, and showcase your expertise to increase your visibility in the market.

3. Utilize Referral Marketing

Word-of-mouth marketing is incredibly valuable. Offer exceptional service to your clients and encourage them to refer your services to others. Consider implementing a referral program that rewards clients for referring new business to you.

4. Leverage Online Advertising

Online advertising can be a cost-effective way to reach your target market. Consider using platforms like Google Ads or social media advertising to target specific demographics and industries. Create compelling ad copy and visuals that highlight your unique offerings and drive potential clients to your website or contact information.

Conclusion

Understanding your target market is the key to building a successful corporate event planning business. By identifying your ideal client, conducting market research, segmenting your market, and using effective marketing strategies, you can attract and engage your target market effectively. In the next chapter, we'll delve into the process of developing a comprehensive business plan to guide your corporate event planning business. Stay tuned!

Chapter 4: Developing Your Business Plan

Creating a comprehensive business plan is a crucial step when starting your corporate event planning business. Think of it as your roadmap, guiding you through the journey, outlining your goals, strategies, and financial projections. But why exactly do you need a business plan, and what should it include? Let's break it down.

Why Do You Need a Business Plan?

A business plan is more than just a document; it's a tool to help you clarify your vision, organize your thoughts, and set a clear direction for your business. It's essential for communicating your ideas to potential investors, lenders, and partners. Plus, a solid business plan helps you anticipate challenges, identify opportunities, and set realistic goals. It's like having a GPS for your entrepreneurial journey, ensuring you stay on track.

Components of a Business Plan

A well-designed business plan typically includes several key components. Let's explore each one in detail:

Executive Summary:

Start with the executive summary. This section provides a high-level overview of your business plan, summarizing the key points and showcasing the strengths of your corporate event planning business. Think of it as your elevator pitch – concise yet compelling.

Company Description:

Here, you'll delve into the details about your corporate event planning business. Outline your mission, vision, and values. Describe the legal structure of your business and highlight any unique aspects or competitive advantages that set you apart in the industry. This section should give a clear picture of what your business is all about.

Market Analysis:

Conducting a thorough market analysis is crucial. Understand the current landscape of the corporate event planning industry, identify your target market, and analyze the demand for event planning services. Research your competition to determine your unique selling points. Knowing the market helps you position your business strategically.

Organization and Management:

Describe the organizational structure of your business. Outline the roles and responsibilities of key team members. Include information about your professional background and qualifications to showcase your expertise in event planning. This section should demonstrate that you have a capable team ready to execute your vision.

Services and Pricing:

Outline the services you'll offer. Be specific about the types of events you'll specialize in and the specific services you'll provide, such as venue selection, budget management, vendor coordination, and event logistics. Determine your pricing strategy and justify it. Clients want to know exactly what they're paying for and why it's worth it.

Marketing and Sales Strategy:

Detail your marketing and sales strategies. Identify your target market and outline your plans for reaching them through various channels, such as digital marketing, networking, referrals, and advertising. Include a sales forecast to project your revenue and growth potential. This section should show how you plan to attract and retain clients.

Financial Projections:

Develop a comprehensive financial plan. Include projected income statements, cash flow statements, and balance sheets. Take into account your start-up costs, overhead expenses, revenue projections, and profitability goals. This section is crucial for demonstrating the financial viability of your business to potential investors or lenders.

Implementation Plan:

Outline your step-by-step plan for launching and operating your business. Include key milestones, target dates, and responsible individuals for each task. This section shows that you have a clear, actionable plan to achieve your goals and execute your strategies.

Risk Analysis:

Evaluate potential risks and challenges that could impact your business. Identify strategies for mitigating those risks and develop contingency plans. Demonstrating that you've considered potential challenges and have plans in place to address them will inspire confidence in potential investors or lenders.

Conclusion

Developing a business plan is a critical step in starting your corporate event planning business. It provides a roadmap for success, helps you communicate your vision and strategies to stakeholders, and is essential for attracting investors, securing financing, and guiding your business toward growth and profitability.

Next Chapter: Legal and Regulatory Considerations

In the next chapter, we'll explore the various legal and regulatory considerations you need to be aware of when starting a corporate event planning business. Understanding these considerations is crucial for ensuring compliance and avoiding potential legal pitfalls. Stay tuned!

Chapter 5: Legal and Regulatory Considerations

Starting your corporate event planning business is exciting, but it's essential to understand the legal and regulatory landscape you'll be navigating. Compliance with these laws not only protects your business but also ensures you deliver a professional and reliable service to your clients. Let's dive into the key legal and regulatory aspects you need to be aware of when starting your corporate event planning business.

Understanding Business Structures

One of the first decisions you'll need to make is choosing the legal structure that best fits your business needs. There are several options to consider:

- **Sole Proprietorship:** This is the simplest structure, where you and your business are one entity. It's easy to set up but offers no personal liability protection.
- **Partnership:** If you're starting the business with someone else, a

partnership might be suitable. It shares the responsibility and profits but also means shared liability.
- **Limited Liability Company (LLC):** This structure offers liability protection while allowing for flexible management and tax options.
- **Corporation:** This is more complex and suits larger businesses. It offers strong liability protection and potential tax benefits but comes with more regulatory requirements.

Each structure has its pros and cons, so it's wise to consult with a legal professional or accountant to determine the best choice for your specific circumstances.

Business Registration and Licensing

After deciding on your business structure, you'll need to register your business with the appropriate government agencies. This usually involves:

- **Registering Your Business Name:** Ensure your business name is unique and legally protected.
- **Obtaining a Tax Identification Number:** This is essential for tax purposes and is often referred to as an

Employer Identification Number (EIN) in the U.S.
- **Applying for Licenses and Permits:** Depending on your location and the nature of your events, you might need specific licenses or permits. Research the requirements in your area to ensure compliance.

Contracts and Agreements

Contracts and agreements are the backbone of the event planning industry. They set clear terms and conditions, protecting both your business interests and your clients. Essential elements to include in your contracts are:

- **Fees and Payment Terms:** Clearly outline your pricing structure and payment schedules.
- **Cancellation Policies:** Define the terms under which either party can cancel the agreement.
- **Liability Clauses:** Protect yourself against potential legal issues.
- **Intellectual Property Rights:** Clarify ownership and usage rights of any creative materials.

Always consult with a legal professional to draft comprehensive and legally sound contracts.

Insurance Coverage

Insurance is crucial to safeguard your business and clients from potential risks and liabilities. Consider the following types of coverage:

- **Liability Insurance:** Protects against claims of bodily injury or property damage.
- **Property Insurance:** Covers damage to your business property or equipment.
- **Professional Indemnity Insurance:** Protects against claims of professional negligence or mistakes.

Research different insurance providers and policies to find the best options for your business.

Intellectual Property Rights

Respecting and protecting intellectual property rights is vital in the event planning industry. This includes using images, logos, and other copyrighted materials with proper authorization. Avoid using third-party materials without permission, as it can lead to legal issues and harm your reputation. Work with a legal professional to ensure you're compliant with intellectual property laws.

Privacy and Data Protection

In today's digital world, privacy and data protection are paramount. As an event planner, you'll likely collect and store personal information about clients, attendees, and vendors. Implement robust data security measures and adhere to privacy regulations such as:

- **General Data Protection Regulation (GDPR):** Applies if you handle data of EU citizens.
- **California Consumer Privacy Act (CCPA):** Relevant if you do business in California.

Understand the specific regulations that apply to your jurisdiction and ensure compliance.

Tax Obligations

Understanding your tax obligations is critical. Work with an accountant or tax professional to ensure you're meeting all tax requirements, including:

- **Maintaining Financial Records:** Keep detailed records of all transactions.
- **Filing Tax Returns:** Ensure timely and accurate filing of your tax returns.

- **Specific Event Planning Taxes:** Be aware of sales taxes for ticketed events or taxes on vendor payments.

Conclusion

Navigating the legal and regulatory considerations is essential for the success and longevity of your corporate event planning business. From choosing the right business structure to complying with licensing requirements and protecting intellectual property, understanding and adhering to these aspects will help you operate ethically, professionally, and within the law. In the next chapter, we'll explore setting up your business operations. Stay tuned!

Chapter 6: Setting Up Your Business Operations

Setting up your business operations is a crucial step in starting a successful corporate event planning business. It involves organizing the various aspects of your business to ensure smooth functioning and efficiency. In this chapter, we will explore the key components of setting up your business operations.

Establishing a Legal Structure

One of the first steps in setting up your business operations is choosing a legal structure for your company. The most common options for a corporate event planning business include sole proprietorship, partnership, limited liability company (LLC), and corporation. Each structure has its own advantages and disadvantages, so it's important to carefully evaluate which one suits your business goals and needs.

Once you have selected a legal structure, you will need to register your business name with the appropriate government authorities. This ensures that your business operates under a unique and legally recognized name. Additionally, you may need to obtain any necessary licenses or permits required by your local jurisdiction to run your corporate event planning business legally.

Establishing Financial Systems

Sound financial management is crucial for the success of any business. As an event planner, you will need to set up financial systems to keep track of income, expenses, and profits. This includes opening a business bank account to separate your personal and business finances. Additionally, investing in accounting software can help you streamline financial management tasks. This software can assist in creating professional invoices, tracking payments, and generating financial reports. By having organized financial systems in place, you can accurately monitor your business's financial health and make informed decisions.

Implementing Operational Processes

Efficient operational processes are vital for running a smooth operation. These processes encompass various aspects of your business, including client onboarding, event planning and execution, vendor management, and post-event evaluation. Creating standard operating procedures (SOPs) for each of these processes will ensure consistency and professionalism in all your operations.

For client onboarding, develop a structured process to gather all necessary information from clients, such as event goals, budget, and preferences. This will help you understand their expectations and deliver tailor-made event experiences.

When it comes to event planning and execution, establish a system for managing event logistics, coordinating with vendors, and overseeing event setup and breakdown. This will help you stay organized and ensure a seamless event experience for your clients and attendees.

Vendor management is another crucial aspect of your business operations. Develop a process for sourcing and evaluating vendors based on their reliability, quality of services, and cost competitiveness. Building strong relationships with trusted vendors will contribute to the success of your events.

Lastly, conducting post-event evaluations allows you to assess the success of your events and identify areas for improvement. Surveying clients and attendees, analyzing event metrics, and documenting lessons learned will help you refine your event planning processes and deliver even better experiences in the future.

Investing in Technology

In today's digital age, investing in technology is essential for streamlining business operations and staying competitive. Consider adopting event management software that can assist in tasks such as event registration, attendee management, and event promotion. This technology can save you time and effort by automating manual processes and providing valuable insights into event performance.

Additionally, having a professional and user-friendly website is crucial for establishing your online presence. Your website should showcase your services, past event portfolios, testimonials, and contact information. Implementing search engine optimization (SEO) strategies will help your website rank higher in search engine results, making it easier for potential clients to find you.

Conclusion

Efficiently setting up your business operations is fundamental to the success of your corporate event planning business. By establishing a legal structure, implementing financial systems, creating operational processes, and investing in technology, you will lay a strong foundation for your business. As you evolve and grow, continuously evaluate and improve your operations to enhance efficiency, deliver exceptional service, and achieve your business goals.

Next Chapter: Legal and Regulatory Considerations

In the next chapter, we will explore the various legal and regulatory considerations that you need to be aware of when starting a corporate event planning business. Understanding these considerations is crucial for ensuring compliance and avoiding potential legal pitfalls.

Chapter 7: Building Your Brand and Online Presence

Building a strong brand and establishing a compelling online presence are essential steps in launching a successful corporate event planning business. Your brand is what sets you apart from competitors and helps potential clients understand what you offer. Meanwhile, your online presence allows you to reach a wider audience and showcase your expertise and services. In this chapter, we will explore strategies for building your brand and creating a robust online presence.

Understanding the Importance of Branding

Branding is much more than just a logo or a catchy tagline. It encompasses the overall perception and reputation of your business. A strong brand conveys professionalism, reliability, and a clear value proposition. It helps potential clients understand what you do, who you serve, and why they should choose your services over others.

To develop a strong brand, start by defining your unique selling proposition (USP). What sets you apart from other event planners? Maybe you have a specific niche or specialize in certain types of events. Identify what makes your services valuable and communicate that in your brand messaging.

Creating a Compelling Brand Identity

Once you have defined your USP, it's time to create a compelling brand identity. This includes designing a logo, choosing a color palette, and establishing a consistent visual style. Your brand identity should reflect your business values and resonate with your target market.

Consider hiring a professional graphic designer to create a visually appealing logo and accompanying brand materials. Your logo should be memorable, versatile, and aligned with your brand's personality. Use your color palette consistently across all marketing materials, including your website, social media profiles, and printed materials.

Building a Professional Website

Your website is often the first point of contact for potential clients, so it's important to make a strong impression. Invest in creating a professional and user-friendly website that showcases your services, testimonials, and past event successes. A well-designed website builds trust and credibility with your target audience.

Ensure that your website is responsive and optimized for mobile devices, as many people access the internet via smartphones and tablets. Make it easy for visitors to contact you by providing clear contact information and a contact form. Regularly update your website with fresh content, including blog posts or case studies, to demonstrate your expertise and keep visitors engaged.

Utilizing Social Media Platforms

Social media platforms provide an excellent opportunity to promote your corporate event planning business and engage with potential clients. Identify which platforms your target audience is most active on and create profiles accordingly. Some popular platforms for event planners include Facebook, Instagram, LinkedIn, and Twitter.

Share valuable content regularly, such as event planning tips, industry news, and success stories. Engage with your followers by responding to comments, answering questions, and participating in relevant discussions. Use social media to showcase your expertise and build relationships with potential clients and industry influencers.

Networking and Collaboration

Networking is essential for building your brand and growing your corporate event planning business. Attend industry events, join professional associations, and participate in online forums to connect with other event planners and potential clients. Collaborate with complementary businesses, such as caterers, venues, and photographers, to expand your network and offer comprehensive services to clients.

Consider hosting your own networking events or educational workshops to establish yourself as a thought leader in the industry. Building relationships and partnerships through networking can lead to valuable referrals and new business opportunities.

Conclusion

Building your brand and establishing a strong online presence are crucial for success in the corporate event planning industry. A well-defined brand identity and a professional website help you stand out from competitors and attract potential clients. Utilizing social media platforms and networking with industry professionals allow you to reach a wider audience and build valuable relationships. Invest time and effort into building your brand and online presence, as they will serve as strong foundations for the growth of your corporate event planning business.

Next chapter: Acquiring Clients and Networking

Chapter 8: Acquiring Clients and Networking

Growing your corporate event planning business hinges on two crucial strategies: acquiring clients and building a robust network. These strategies not only help you attract new clients but also establish valuable partnerships that contribute to the success of your business.

Identifying Your Ideal Clients

Before diving into client acquisition, it's important to clearly identify your ideal client. This focus helps streamline your marketing efforts and tailor your services to meet specific needs. Think about the size of the companies you want to work with, the industries they operate in, and the types of events they typically host. By understanding your target market and ideal clients, you can craft targeted marketing messages and strategies that resonate with them.

Building Your Network

Networking is a powerful tool in the event planning industry. It's not just about who you know, but who knows you. Attending industry events, conferences, and trade shows can be incredibly beneficial. These venues provide opportunities to meet potential clients and industry professionals face-to-face. Joining professional organizations and associations related to event planning can further expand your network and enhance your credibility.

In today's digital world, online networking platforms like LinkedIn are indispensable. Connect with professionals in your industry, join relevant groups, and actively participate in discussions. This will help showcase your expertise and build relationships with potential clients and partners.

Referral Marketing

Referrals are a goldmine for event planners. Happy clients are likely to recommend your services to their colleagues and business contacts. Deliver exceptional customer service and successful events to encourage referrals. Don't be shy about asking satisfied clients to refer you. Consider implementing a referral program that rewards clients for recommending your services. This can motivate them to spread the word about your business.

Online Advertising

Online advertising is another highly effective strategy for acquiring clients. Platforms like Google Ads and social media sites offer targeted advertising options. Develop compelling ad copy and creative visuals that highlight your unique selling proposition and attract potential clients. Online ads can be tailored to reach your specific target audience, ensuring that your message gets in front of the right people.

Content Marketing

Content marketing involves creating valuable and relevant content to attract and engage your target audience. This can take the form of blog posts, articles, videos, and downloadable resources related to corporate event planning. Share your expertise, offer tips and insights, and showcase your past events. Establish yourself as a trusted authority in the industry. Distribute your content through your website, social media channels, and email marketing campaigns to maximize its reach and impact.

Strategic Partnerships

Establishing strategic partnerships with related businesses can be mutually beneficial. Identify businesses that offer complementary services, such as catering companies, venues, photographers, and audiovisual providers. Collaborate with these businesses to offer package deals or cross-promote each other's services. This not only expands your reach but also provides added value to your clients.

Conclusion

Acquiring clients and building a strong network are fundamental for the growth and success of your corporate event planning business. By identifying your ideal clients, networking with industry professionals, implementing referral marketing and online advertising strategies, utilizing content marketing, and establishing strategic partnerships, you can attract new clients and position yourself as a leading event planner in your industry. Consistent effort in acquiring clients and networking will drive the sustainable growth of your business.

Next Chapter: Legal and Regulatory Considerations

In the next chapter, we'll dive into the various legal and regulatory considerations you need to be aware of when starting a corporate event planning business. Understanding these considerations is crucial for ensuring compliance and avoiding potential legal pitfalls. Stay tuned!

Chapter 9: Providing Exceptional Client Service

Welcome to Chapter 9 of our journey on how to build a successful corporate event planning business. This chapter is all about mastering the art of providing exceptional client service. Trust me, outstanding client service is crucial. It not only enhances your reputation but also leads to client satisfaction and loyalty, which are the foundations of a thriving business. Let's dive into the strategies and best practices for delivering top-notch client service in the event planning industry.

Understanding Your Clients' Needs and Expectations

The cornerstone of exceptional client service is understanding your clients' needs and expectations. This means honing your communication and active listening skills to ensure you're capturing every detail. Here's how to do it:

Conduct Thorough Client Consultations

Before each event, take the time to conduct in-depth client consultations. Ask detailed questions, listen attentively, and take copious notes. You want to understand their vision for the event, budget constraints, preferences, and any specific requirements. This will give you valuable insights and set a strong foundation for the planning process.

Maintain Open Lines of Communication

Throughout the event planning process, keep the lines of communication open with your clients. Regular check-ins, progress updates, and seeking their input on key decisions will foster a sense of collaboration and ensure their expectations are being met. This ongoing dialogue is essential for building trust and delivering a successful event.

Creating Customized Event Experiences

Every client has unique goals and objectives for their corporate event. To provide exceptional service, you need to create customized experiences that align with their vision. Here's how:

Tailor Your Approach

Use the information gathered during your client consultation to tailor your event planning approach. Consider their preferences for venue, decor, catering, entertainment, and any specific requirements they may have. By personalizing the event experience, you demonstrate your attention to detail and dedication to meeting their specific needs.

Show Your Creativity

Bring your creative flair to the table by suggesting unique ideas that match your client's vision. Whether it's a bespoke theme, innovative decor, or interactive elements, showing your creativity can elevate the event and exceed client expectations.

Providing Clear and Transparent Communication

Clear and transparent communication is key to building trust with your clients. Here's how to keep them informed and engaged throughout the planning process:

Use Project Management Tools

Utilize project management tools or software to share important documents, event details, and progress updates with your clients. This not only streamlines communication but also serves as a centralized platform for collaboration.

Be Proactive and Responsive

Address any concerns or questions raised by your clients promptly. Provide clear explanations or solutions to their queries. Regularly seek feedback throughout the event planning process to show your commitment to their satisfaction and make timely adjustments if needed.

Going Above and Beyond

To truly stand out, look for opportunities to exceed your clients' expectations. Here's how to go the extra mile:

Add Personal Touches

Consider providing personalized touches or surprises during the event. This could be anything from unique event signage to customized gift bags for attendees. These small gestures demonstrate your attention to detail and commitment to delivering an exceptional event experience.

Be Present and Attentive

During the event itself, be present and attentive to your clients' needs. Ensure everything is running smoothly and address any concerns immediately. Strive to anticipate their needs and address them proactively.

Handling Challenges and Resolving Issues

Even with meticulous planning, challenges and issues can arise during events. How you handle these situations can significantly impact client satisfaction and their perception of your business. Here's how to manage them effectively:

Stay Calm and Professional

When faced with challenges, remain calm and maintain a professional demeanor. Communicate openly with your clients, keeping them informed about the situation and the steps you are taking to resolve it. Offer alternative solutions and work closely with your team, suppliers, and vendors to rectify the situation as quickly as possible.

Conduct Post-Event Evaluations

After the event, conduct a post-event evaluation and seek feedback from your clients. Use this feedback as an opportunity for continuous improvement, making necessary adjustments to enhance future event experiences.

Conclusion: Building Client Relationships through Exceptional Service

Providing exceptional client service is not just about executing flawless events; it's about building strong and lasting relationships with your clients. By understanding their needs and expectations, customizing event experiences, communicating transparently, going above and beyond, and handling challenges effectively, you will develop a strong reputation for providing exceptional service in the corporate event planning industry.

In the next chapter, we will explore strategies for growing your corporate event planning business. Stay tuned!

Chapter 10: Growing Your Corporate Event Planning Business

Growing your corporate event planning business is one of the most exciting and crucial phases of your entrepreneurial journey. It's a time to implement strategies that will help you expand your client base, increase revenue, and take your business to new heights. In this chapter, we'll dive into various tactics to foster business growth.

Expanding Your Service Offerings

One effective way to grow your corporate event planning business is by expanding the services you offer. Think about adding new services that complement your existing ones or branching into different areas of event planning. Here are a few ideas:

- **Venue Sourcing and Negotiations:** Offer comprehensive venue selection services to help clients find the perfect location for their event while ensuring they get the best possible deal.
- **Event Technology Solutions:** Incorporate event management

software, mobile apps, or registration systems to enhance the event experience and streamline processes for your clients.
- **Event Marketing and Promotion:** Assist clients with event marketing by offering services like social media promotion, email marketing campaigns, and content creation.

By diversifying your service offerings, you can attract new clients with different needs and preferences, and add more value to your existing client base.

Building Strong Referral Networks

Referrals are invaluable in the event planning industry. Happy clients are often your best marketing tool, as they will recommend your services to their network, leading to new business opportunities. To build a strong referral network:

- **Deliver Exceptional Service:** Consistently exceeding client expectations increases the likelihood that they will recommend your services to others.
- **Cultivate Relationships with Vendors and Suppliers:** Establishing strong relationships with vendors and

suppliers can lead to referrals, as they may recommend you to their clients.
- **Collaborate with Complementary Businesses:** Partnering with businesses that offer complementary services, like caterers, photographers, or entertainment providers, can result in mutual referrals and shared marketing efforts.

Implementing Targeted Marketing Strategies

Effective marketing is crucial for growing your corporate event planning business. By implementing targeted marketing strategies, you can reach your ideal clients and stand out from the competition. Consider the following tactics:

- **Develop a Compelling Brand Story and Unique Selling Proposition (USP):** Your brand story and USP should resonate with your target audience and clearly communicate what sets you apart.
- **Create Engaging Content:** Use your website and social media platforms to showcase your expertise and highlight successful events you've planned. Make sure the content is visually appealing and engaging.

- **Utilize Search Engine Optimization (SEO)**: Improve your website's visibility in search engine results to attract more organic traffic.
- **Invest in Online Advertising**: Platforms like Google Ads and social media offer targeted advertising options. Develop compelling ads to attract potential clients.
- **Participate in Industry Events**: Attend trade shows, conferences, and other industry events to network with potential clients and professionals.
- **Leverage Email Marketing**: Use email campaigns to stay connected with existing clients and nurture leads.

Offering Specialized Event Planning Services

To differentiate yourself from competitors and attract clients looking for specific expertise, consider offering specialized event planning services. Some potential niches include:

- **Sustainable Event Planning**: Cater to environmentally conscious clients by offering services like eco-friendly vendor sourcing, waste reduction strategies, and carbon offset programs.
- **Technology-Driven Events**: Specialize in planning

technology-focused events, such as product launches, conferences, or trade shows, for clients in the tech industry.
- **Corporate Team Building Events**: Develop unique team-building event concepts that promote teamwork, leadership, and employee engagement.

By offering specialized services, you position yourself as an expert in your niche and appeal to clients who require specific event planning expertise.

Establishing an Online Presence

In today's digital age, having a strong online presence is essential for business growth. Here are some key steps:

- **Create a Professional Website**: Your website should showcase your portfolio, services, and client testimonials. Make sure it's user-friendly and professional.
- **Optimize for Search Engines**: Use SEO strategies to increase your website's visibility and attract more visitors.
- **Leverage Social Media**: Use platforms like Facebook, Instagram, and LinkedIn to share industry insights,

promote your services, and engage with potential clients.
- **Publish Valuable Content**: Create blog posts, videos, and other content that educates and entertains your target audience. This positions you as a thought leader in the industry.
- **Encourage Client Reviews**: Ask satisfied clients to leave reviews on platforms like Google My Business or Yelp. Positive reviews build credibility and attract new clients.

By effectively utilizing online platforms, you can increase brand awareness, reach a wider audience, and establish yourself as a reputable event planning professional.

Conclusion

Growing your corporate event planning business requires a thoughtful and strategic approach. By expanding your service offerings, building strong referral networks, implementing targeted marketing strategies, offering specialized services, and establishing an online presence, you can position your business for success. Continuously adapt and refine your growth strategies to meet the changing needs of your clients and stay ahead of the competition in the dynamic world of event planning.

Next Chapter: Legal and Regulatory Considerations

In the next chapter, we will explore the various legal and regulatory considerations you need to be aware of when starting a corporate event planning business. Understanding these considerations is crucial for ensuring compliance and avoiding potential legal pitfalls. Stay tuned!

www.ingramcontent.com/pod-product-compliance
Lightning Source LLC
Chambersburg PA
CBHW070133230526
45472CB00004B/1523